USA First-Class

BIG AMERICAN TRIP

USA First-Class

Big American Trip

Shearsman Books / Exeter

First published in the United Kingdom in 2007
by Shearsman Books Ltd
58 Velwell Road
Exeter EX4 4LD

ISBN 978-1-84861-015-6
First Edition

USA First-Class

FOR E

Blaine, WA, home of the US-Canada Peace Arch was named by Cain Bros., townsite proprietors, in 1884, only twenty-five years after it was first settled as Semiahmoo, the name of the tribe of Salish Indians who inhabited Semiahmoo Bay until being relocated to the 390 (presently 320) acre reservation.

USA First-Class

GOOD ENGLISH IS "FILL HER UP"

In Texaco it is said "they"
are forcing the coast to a single state
from Tijuana to Vancouver.

It is the common feeling,
the agreement of the convenience store.

"Labatts or Dos Equis," dice hermano
sin sleeves, "same shit, different language."

Chevron Corporation
6001 Bollinger Canyon Rd.
San Ramon, CA 94583
United States

Raspberry fields, Lynden WA. Washington State leads the nation in red raspberry production. In 2004, Washington raised 60.3 million pounds of red raspberries valued at $46.6 million.

USA First-Class

MARGIN LESSON

"THAT" IS THE DEFINING, OR RESTRICTIVE, PRONOUN, "WHICH" THE NONDEFINING, OR NONRESTRICTIVE.

- WASHINGTON STATE RASPBERRIES, WHICH ARE HARVESTED BY ILLEGAL ALIENS, ARE DELICIOUS.

- WASHINGTON STATE RASPBERRIES THAT ARE HARVESTED BY ILLEGAL ALIENS ARE DELICIOUS.

WASHINGTON STATE
RASPBERRY COMMISSION
1626 N. ATLANTIC
SPOKANE, WA 99205

Snoqualmie Falls, with its 270-foot cascade of water, one of the state's most-visited attractions, is most widely recognized as the setting for the groundbreaking television series, "Twin Peaks." Snoqualmie is an English variation of "sah-KOH-koh" and "Sdob-dwahibbluh," Salish words meaning "moon."

USA First-Class

THE EMPHASIS IN ENGLISH
IS RELIGIOUSLY IN THE POSSESSIONS
BUT THE ADORATION OF THE SALISH
IS IN A TENDER PLACE.

FOR EXAMPLE, THE SALISH PENETRATE
THEIR RIFLES WITH A CLEANING ROD
IS EXPRESSED : "DIRECTING A MOVABLE DRY POINT
OF THE HOLLOW BY MEANS OF A TOOL."

ACCORDING TO DOROTHY LEE, "THE HUNTER
WHO HAS LOST HIS LUCK DOES NOT SAY
'I CANNOT KILL DEER ANYMORE,'
BUT 'DEER DO NOT WANT ANYMORE TO DIE FOR ME.'"

WEYERHAEUSER COMPANY
35131 SE DOUGLAS ST
STE 112
SNOQUALMIE, WA
98065-1233

Available Non-Management Positions

Heist Cream Parlor Attendant - Greet customers, serve ice cream and fudge to guests, operate cash register, follow proper sanitation procedures.

Buffalo Burger - Take and prepare food orders, use flat top grill and fryer, serve food orders over the counter to customers, follow proper sanitation procedures.

General Catering - Accommodate special events including the Pitchfork Fondue, follow proper sanitation procedures.

Rough Rider Motel Customer Service Rep - Check in guests at motel front desk, familiarize them to Wenatchee, respond positively to guest questions and concerns, present guests with the opportunity to purchase Musical and Fondue tickets, attraction passes, etc, take reservations, direct incoming phone calls.

Wranglers - Give guests informative, guided trail rides through the desert, ride in the Wenatchee

---

OPPORTUNITY IN WENATCHEE! (HASTA QUE LA PUEBLO ES CERRADO.)

POSTCARD

U.S. DEPARTMENT OF LABOR
200 CONSTITUTION AVE., NW
WASHINGTON, DC 20210

USA First-Class

The Clymer Museum in historic downtown Ellensburg, WA—Return to a time and place where simplicity of life, pioneer spirit, and American values were the cornerstones of the day. The Clymer Museum hosts the permanent collection of John Ford Clymer, who illustrated covers for America's beloved *Saturday Evening Post* and *Look* magazines and created advertising for some of America's best and brightest corporations.

THE REST AREA PASSED OF RYEGRASS WEST
SWALLOWS I-90 WITNESS OF RAINER — ONLY SNOW
TO CENTER THIS LANDSCAPE A NEW BURNING TECHNIQUE
IN THE PLAIN:

SPOKANE 160 MILES

CLYMER MUSEUM OF ART
416 NORTH PEARL
ELLENSBURG, WA 98926

THE STATION OF THE CLASSICAL ROCK ALLOWS
THE FOREIGNER & IS GOOD TOO, WHAT I HEAR:

HOP LOADED

WHALE, I'M HOP LOADED
CZECH IN SEA

ZYGOTE A VIVA
OR 103

MAMA/BABY/TOUCAN
DOOM OR THE DANCE

ON HOP LOADED!
ON HOP LOADED!

WABC RADIO
~~77WABC~~
2 PENN PLAZA
NY, NY 10121

Superior, Montana offers a break from interstate travel as well as an introduction to area history, thanks to the Mineral County Museum. In 1869 the discovery of gold on Cedar Creek by L.A. Barrette created an immediate "stampede" to the area. Among the first to arrive were merchants and businessmen from Frenchtown and Hellgate—now Missoula—considered "one of the most lawful and organized of all gold rushes."

USA First-Class

"The highway is for gamblers—better use your sense."

Camped dry in a cove, 66 miles to Missoula.
This car resists cooperation and I am enormous cramps.

Superior is good name for town lake, but coffee
here is only the brown water.

I am finding very difficult to maintain the 75 mph.

¿ Great terror is the use of the law:
An eager representative of the Cherokee Jeep
patrolled my routine encampment. His duty
the hat and the nod—and the raised eyebrow.

Montana Parks Dept.
1420 E 6th Ave.
PO Box 200701
Helena, MT
59620-0701

Sagebrush. You can identify sagebrush easily by its sharp odor, especially after rain. Early pioneers traveling along the Oregon Trail described the scent as "a medicinal yet whore-like mixture of turpentine and camphor."

USA First-Class

SAYS THE ALIEN JAMAKE HIGHWATER:

IT IS NOT SIMPLY A MATTER OF LANGUAGE...
IT IS POSSIBLE TO TRANSLATE WITH FAIR
ACCURACY FROM ONE LANGUAGE TO ANOTHER
WITHOUT LOSING TOO MUCH OF THE ORIGINAL
MEANING. BUT THERE ARE NO METHODS
BY WHICH WE CAN TRANSLATE A MENTALITY
AND ITS ALIEN IDEAS.

TO WHOM IT MAY CONCERN

POSTCARD

ENTIENDA MAL = MISSVERSTEHEN SIE

MISUNDERSTAND "THE SAGE AS BRUSH"

MISUNDERSTAND "THE HORIZON AS LONGING OF LENGTH AND DEPTH"

MISUNDERSTAND "BARBED WIRE AS ABSENCE"

MISUNDERSTAND "PRESENCE AS ABSENCE OF BARBED WIRE"

MISUNDERSTAND "WE" AS "IN THIS TOGETHER"

MISUNDERSTAND "CONFLICT" AS "CONFLICT"

USA First-Class

_____

_____

TRAGEDY ASSISTANCE
PROGRAM FOR SURVIVORS
NATIONAL HEADQUARTERS
1621 CONNECTICUT AVE. NW
SUITE 300
WASHINGTON, DC 20001

USA First-Class

MONTANA OF THE IMPULSE DISABLES TO DEFECATE THE MORNING—
TIME TAUNTING OF THE MOUNTAIN. MONTANA OF THE SUN DROP DEW,
NEEDLES OF THE PINE, SHOTS IN MY EYES. MONTANA OF SPEED LIMIT
OF 80 MILES OF THE HOUR MY CAR LAMENTS THE STRUGGLE TO OBTAIN.

MONTANA, "BIG SKY COUNTRY." MONTANA OF THE LIMITLESS
FEAR. MONTANA OF THE "GOD KNOWS WHAT" UNIFORM
FANTASIES, SUV POLICE, SAD HUNTING-ACCIDENT NEWS.

MONTANA OF THE GOD SPITEFUL, MY HOODED DESTINY...
MONTANA, YOU ARE DIFFICULT TO SEE. YOU ARE WET
CRYSTALS OF THE SUN. MONTANA OF CLARK FORKS
AND NO END OF MILES. MONTANA, I AM NOT TO CRY.

MONTANA TOURISM
& PROMOTION DIVISION
301 S PARK AVE
HELENA MT 59601

USA First-Class

EXIT SURPASSED FOR ___?___. MOVE TO LEFT LANE
FOR RUGGED FORD TRUCK OF THE U.S. COLORS BRANDED SHERIFF.

BUT THIS TIME I ATTEMPT A DIVERSE APPROACH. I INCLINE MY ELBOW
IN THE OPEN WINDOW AND POSITION MY PALM TO MY CHIN, HIDING
WITH EFFECTIVENESS MY UNPERSONLY FACE — AS IF OUTSIDE I WAS SIMPLY
"GOING AND GOING" — OH, LIKE ANY QUEER HAIR FLAPPING THROUGH
THIS STATE TO ANOTHER ENDLESS.

I PRAYED, "INVISIBLE ENERGIES, TRIGGER THIS MY LUCK!"

& THANK YOU, IT WAS NOT IN EXCESS. HE RETREATED,
STRUCK SUDDENLY TO HIS LIGHTS.

HE IS TODAY FOR SOMEONE ELSE TRUE COLORS OF THE PROBLEM.

[AMIGOS]

THE RIGHT OF WAY:

I COME TOO FAST OR SLOW & THIS UPSETS YOU.

A WIND BLEW OUT MY LIGHT AND IT BURNS YOU.

[I TALK NOW. BUT I WILL TREMBLE. BEFORE YOUR GUN I WILL SAY "YOUR NOUN IS MY VERB, SIR."]

MISSOULA POLICE DEPT.
435 PYMAN STREET
MISSOULA, MT 57802

USA First-Class

At the Seeley Lake Campground, with its huge Tamaracks (Western larch) festooned with long drapes of Grandfather's beard lichen, the "unearthly howl" of the loon adds a sense of mystery to the hills. Thoreau observed the loon's call: "sounds more like that of a wolf than any bird."

USA First-Class

THERE IS A STRETCH BEFORE MISSOULA: EXTENSIVE
GMO VALLEY, GREEN ROAD SIGN, EXIT 61: "TARKIO."

ELK ON THE ROOF RACK, DOS BLANCOS SMOKE CIGARS.

THIS IS SWITCHBACK? THIS IS ZIGZAG?

CROSSING THE MOUNTAIN AGAIN LOST OF TREES
THE HAWK IS THE BLUR OF THE HOMELESS HELLO.

I NEED TO RECALL THE TRAIN OF THE NEGATIVE LOAD,
THE DESPERATION WHICH I AM TO EXPERIMENT: STRIP MINING
THE CAMOUFLAGE UNIFORMS IN LANDSCAPE ANGELIC OF MONTANA.

KARYNA MCGLYNN
HOLLYWOOD TRAILER COURT
1700 COOLEY STREET
MISSOULA, MT 59802

USA First-Class

THE NEW BREED

IT THINKS ACCORDING TO THE ISOLATED THING, NOT THE CORRELATED THING.
THE PICKUP TRUCK IS ALONE IN THE MUD HOLE. THERE IS NO BIKINIS.

IT IS THEIR BOOTS ARE TOO TIGHT.
IT IS THEIR PANTS ARE TOO BLUE.
THE STIFF PAY TO BE HARDER.
     —AND THEY ARE SAVED

IS THEIRS NO FUNCTION BUT TO CLUSTER PATTERNS
OF LABOR? FOR AUCTION? FOR ARMIES AND MUSEUMS?

Montana Right To Life Assn.
1700 N Last Chance Gulch
Suite C
Helena, MT 57601

POSTCARD

HAND IN THE MATTER (1)

ALWAYS THE ONE THAT STABS AN IMMENSE
SYSTEM CONFUSED OF SYSTEMS:
DOLOR A CABEZA, REMOVE MY EYES!
IT IS THE HAND THAT CAN GROPE MY HEART
TORN OF THE CENTER OF THE SYSTEM I FLEE.
GOD, IT AVOIDS ME. DONDE ESTA ...
LAND, TREES, BUILDINGS SERVE NOT THEIR SUBJECTS.
& SUCH TIES MY HAND.
THE SYSTEMIC HOMOGENEITY, CLASSES
OF COMFY PHENOMENA. TRACKS
OF THE SURFACE OF UNDERLYING PROCESSES.
IT DISABLES MY HAND.
A RIVER NOT A RIVER, BUT A CONNECTION
OR CIRCUIT OF THE HYDROLOGY: A MEANS.

TO WHOM IT MAY CONCERN

The town of Three Forks is easily accessible off I-90, US-287, and Montana Highway 2 and lies enroute between Yellowstone National Park and Glacier National Park. There are numerous recreational opportunities, superb fishing and hunting, and the Headwaters Public Golf Course features a 9-hole course against a background of scenic panoramas!

ALL IS ROCK ERODED AND THE PLANNED OBSOLESCENCE.
NO PLANS TO GROW: BLANK HILL OF LIMP SAPLINGS,
OR ROBUST PLANTS OF THE MUTATED SEED.
THE LABORERS WHITEWASHED FROM THE VIEW:

NO FACILITIES

BROKE BOTTLE KING OF BEERS.
ANONYMOUS POST, THE FLAG IN THE GUARDRAIL

DEPT. OF TRANSPORTATION
2880 SKYWAY DRIVE
HELENA MT 57602

POSTCARD

Says the alien Terence McKenna:

"The starships of the future,
in other words the vehicles of the future,
which will explore the high frontier
of the unknown, will be syntactical.
The engineers of the future will be poets."

NASA / DOD
Ames Research Center
Mountain View, CA 94035

Eagle Bend Golf Course in Big Fork, MT. With first-class resorts, elegant country clubs and delightful "country" courses, Montana is a great place to spend your golfing vacation—although there is always the hazard of being distracted by the stunning scenery or by daydreams of fly-fishing and big-game hunting!

PLAIN ENGLISH

BEST ESTIMATION IS 50 MILES IN FRONT OF ME:

SAGE BRUSH IN GRAY ROCK.

DRIED SNAKE ON THE ROADSIDE.

SENATOR CONRAD BURNS
116 WEST FRONT STREET
MISSOULA, MT 59802

Downtown Big Timber, MT. Stroll down Main Street and you'll find friendly people and inviting shops. Ullman's Lumber is owned and operated by the 3rd and 4th generations of Ullmans. Montana-made gifts, western jeans, hardware, health foods, restaurants, and sports supplies are all within walking distance. Enjoy small town pleasures such as a 1930s soda fountain, antique shops, or just a shady bench to watch the world go by.

YO NO DESEO QUE EL MUNDO SE IRIA
YO NO DESEO MIRAR EL MUNDO SALEN

I DO NOT WISH THAT THE WORLD WOULD GO BY
I DO NOT WISH TO WATCH THE WORLD LEAVE

SWEET GRASS COUNTY
CHAMBER OF COMMERCE
& VISITORS CENTER
P.O. BOX 1012
BIG TIMBER, MT 59011

USA First-Class

AND HOW IS CITY "BIG TIMBER" WITH NO TREE?
(SIX MILES MORE, THE TRUTH: "GRAY CLIFF.")

DESIRE THAT HAD BAD GRASS.
THERE IS NOTHING DOES.
WINDMILL STILL IN THE SHUTDOWN:
THE LABORERS ERASED.

YOUR GOD IS ONLY ONE IN THE AFTERNOON.
THE WORSE HEAT IS TO COME.

SWEET GRASS COUNTY
CHAMBER OF COMMERCE
& VISITORS CENTER
P.O. BOX 1012
BIG TIMBER, MT 57011

POSTCARD

KOA "Franchise" in Iraq

Billings, Montana (KOA News) – A bout of homesickness has led to the creation of Kampgrounds of America's newest "franchise" in Iraq.

Lt. Col. Michael Morone, a National Guard neurosurgeon stationed at Camp Babylon in Southern Iraq, was missing the camping trips he would have been taking this spring with his wife, Sally, and their children Ella, 6, and Benjamin, 4. His favorite campground was the KOA in his hometown of Billings, Montana (also the home of KOA's corporate headquarters).

Morone and a few of his friends decided to rename their tent village in Iraq "KOA Babylon," and even constructed their own campground sign.

"We live in tents and trailers here so it is like a campground," said Morone when he emailed KOA headquarters in Billings. "Unfortunately, this summer I will miss spending time at KOA Campground #1 in Billings."

A general surgeon from Hawaii hand-painted a KOA sign that is realistic down to the bright yellow background and unusual reddish tint and the registration mark that signify KOA. The portable sign moves from spot to spot in the camp.

"We're going to treat them like a real KOA franchise," said Mike Gast, KOA's director of communications. "They've been having a lot of fun with it, so we are, too."

"The KOA sign just makes us feel like we are camping back at home," Morone said. "We have some things here that may interest campers. They include fishing in the Euphrates River, a patio to sit on and enjoy your dinner, a volleyball court, gymnasium, one of Saddam's palaces and the Babylon Ruins."

TO WHOM IT MAY CONCERN

SAYS THE ALIEN PA-TA SHAN-JEN:

The brush

MAY PAINT THE MOUNTAINS AND STREAMS

THOUGH THE TERRITORY IS LOST

POSTCARD

USA First-Class

HAND IN THE MATTER (2)

O, TRANSPORT, FOISTING CERTAIN VOLUMES
OF MATERIAL UNDER MY NATIVE TARIFF,
WITHIN "PRESCRIBED" SEGMENTS OF A CYCLE—
TODO TRIES TO SLICE OFF MY HAND.
⋮ O, SUCH A GOD REQUIRES "THE FORCE," DEMANDS
ALTERING THE EARTH IN A CONSTANT
⋮ CALCULABLE WAY. THE TREES RETURN SOMEWHERE,
FAR FROM US. OR NO. ALL THE SPECIES,
DIMENSION, COLOR—ERASURE, ONLY
THE CHEMICAL FACTORIES LEAD
BY THE RADIATE ⋮ GOOD-NATURE OF THE SUN.
BIOLOGICAL TRANSFORMING THE INTERCHANGE
OF THE ENERGY : ALL IS AVOIDED. HERE IS NO
NARRATIVE: BETWEEN LITHOSPHERE AND ATMOSPHERE
OF IMITATION, IS THIS "LYRIC" "BODY" OF "WORK"

TO WHOM IT MAY CONCERN

Little Bighorn Battlefield National Monument memorializes the site of the Battle of the Little Bighorn in which 210 US Cavalrymen, led by Colonel George A. Custer, were wiped out by Sioux and Northern Cheyenne warriors. Bus tours of the battlefield operate from Memorial Day weekend through Labor Day. During the off-season a 17-minute documentary film is shown at the visitor center.

USA First-Class

FEARED VACILLATING LIKE TO SLOW MY AUTO IN CUSTER,
BUT FOR MY LOVE OF OIL I STOPPED. O, FOREBODING WIND—
CAUTIOUS IN ITS LIMITS I VERIFIED: THE CITY NO EXIST.
NO CHILDREN BUT DOGS SCORCH THE BUILDINGS HOLLOW.

ASPHALT OF POTHOLE SCRAP GLASS I NEED AVOID
SLOW IN THE DUST. AND MEASURED ALSO BY THE STEEL
OUTHOUSE SCREWED ON A LATE GARAGE—HERE DISCARDED
AUTOS OF THE DECADES.

THE WAREHOUSE EMPTY, ALL OCTANES EXHAUSTED.

IT IS A TRAP WAITING—
FLIES ON THE POSSUM, THE DOG WITH THREE LEGS—
IT IS INTUITION, HOT AND DRY.

CHEVRON CORPORATION
6001 BOLLINGER CANYON RD.
SAN RAMON, CA 94583

POSTCARD

On "Excuse Us":

Everything "we meant to say," the memorial misplaced or ill sign, or between us language, is the most common and important means to the cooperation.

It is / what / we will never forget?

Hon. ~~Clarence Thomas~~
Hon. ~~Samuel Alito~~
U.S. Supreme Court
U.S. Supreme Court Bldg.
Washington, DC 20543

POSTCARD

FOUND ROADSIDE A WHITE GIRL IS RASTA. HER MANTRA: "IT'S ALL GOOD." SHE IMPARTS A KNOWLEDGE OF THE FOREIGNER TO LEAVE ME A WONDER OF SELF-SCRUTINY.

HOT BLOODED

WELL, I'M HOT BLOODED
CHECK AND SEE

I GOT A FEVER
OF 103

COME ON, BABY,
YOU CAN DO MORE THAN
DANCE

I'M HOT-BLOODED!
HOT-BLOODED!

MORE APPROPRIATES THE DESERT. EVEN IF DULL WORDS.

USA First-Class

WABC RADIO
77WABC
2 PENN PLAZA
NY, NY 10121

HAND IN THE MATTER (3)

IS NOT THE CO-OP SHOPPER, THE BROKEN LOVER—
A DYNAMIC BALANCE OF HOMELY PROCESSES

CONSTRUCTED OF SILENCE, THE BAMBOO LAWN CHAIR,
THE WIND ANNULLED—THE "LYRIC" IS

WRITTEN WITH A HAND OF THE TREMOR
[BLOWN FROM PACIFIC SAND]

IS NO MATTER

POSTCARD

FORCED TO CRAWL IN 10 MILES UNDER—CONSTRUCTION
HIGHWAY IMPLYING WHITE TROOPS PROVIDE LIGHT.

GOD IS DOWN, FEELING THE BEARING ON MY NECK,
BUT I AM UNTIL NOW UNSEEN.

I WAIT. I HIDE BEHIND THE TRAILER—"JUST 18 WHEELS
BETWEEN YOU AND ME, 'GOOD BUDDY'"—

FLAG AFLUTTER THE STEAMROLLER UP AHEAD . . .

NATIONAL SECURITY ADVISOR
THE WHITE HOUSE
1600 PENNSYLVANIA AVE. NW
WASHINGTON, DC 20500

POSTCARD

East of Sweet Briar Lake, a statue of the cow.
Judging the trees and farm below, is eighty feet
in height? Perhaps is first cow—Titan or Totem.

Or is just Test Cow—Tub of the hormone stew.
Company Teet.

No. It is only enormous cow.
I need only enormous cow.

Memoir: need also a future pilgrimage.
If I have love again and propose this holy sight,
they too may have a cow.

Ernesto Mumia Sioux Blanco
En Alguna
Parte En El Futuro

POSTCARD

USA First-Class

AMERICAN
METEOROLOGICAL SOCIETY
1120 G STREET, NW
SUITE 800
WASHINGTON, DC
20005-3826

LIGHTNING!

GOD WOULD MY SEAT YOUR ELECTRIC CHAIR!
THANK YOU, RUBBER, AND AFTER, WHAT?
A SINGLE CLOUD AT LEAST TEN BRUISED MILES
TO TRAVERSE, THE EYE FIRE FUSED IN ROSE.
GREAT LAKES SWALLOW THE LAKE STATES.
HEAVEN A BROKEN PORCH LIGHT FOR THE TRAVELER:
"FOREVER" IS NIGHT HERE, WELCOME HOME.

POSTCARD

The DRIVE is "Welcome to" and "Thank you"

The drive is bison disappear to the hills

The drive is abandoned, condom in the rest area

The Drive is no backyard hill or stump

The DRIVE is find the long definition home

The drive is steel ፧ tar ፧ oil ፧ gas ፧ coffee

The drive is under the weather as under the law

The drive is beyond me

The drive is heartland into stone

USA First-Class

Recreation Vehicle Assn.
3930 University Drive
Fairfax, VA 22030

POSTCARD

[FOR PURPOSES
OF THE DOCUMENTATION]

ROAD SIGN:

TEST SITES NEXT THREE MILES

This is "EXPLANATION."

TWENTY MILES TO FARGO
OR THE TIME IS DISAPPEARED.

Minnesota is home to five professional sports teams, the oldest continuously running theater, one of the largest peat bogs in the country, 10,000 lakes (not including Garrison Keillor's fictional Lake Wobegon), Bob Dylan, and the biggest mall in the country— The Mall of America!

USA First-Class

DULUTH IS 78 MILES BUT WAS ONLY 63.
THE WEATHER HAS KIDNAPPED ME AGAIN.

HERE IT IS WHERE WE TRANSPIRE—CORRIDOR PINES,
THE LOW DOWN SUN, LONG SHADES THAT HAIL.
THE SQUINT. THE SWERVE. HOW COULD WE RETURN?

IT IS THE WET DARK WHERE THE ALIEN CAN DISAPPEAR.
IT IS THE RED LIGHT OF BRAKES, THE STOPPED TRUCK,
THE RAIN OF "NO FEAR." IT IS THE ROADSIDE HORROR
AND I AM THE FEMALE ALONE.

(NOTE: BUY CALCULATOR IN ADDITION A NEW RADIO.)

MINNESOTA DEPARTMENT
OF TRANSPORTATION
375 JOHN IRELAND BLVRD.
SAINT PAUL, MN 55155

POSTCARD

USA First-Class

EXIT 209 IS "STURGEON LAKE"

SIDE OF THE HIGHWAY IS EXPLODED COYOTE

MINNESOTA DEPARTMENT
OF TRANSPORTATION
375 JOHN IRELAND BLVRD.
SAINT PAUL, MN 55155

POSTCARD

DOMINANT NARRATIVES (LOCAL CHAPTER):

WHO SEES ALL SORROWFUL HANDLING, BANDAGING CHEAPLY WITH NO
CARE FOR THE ALIEN LUMP? IT IS THE REMOVE OF THE FACTORY SCHOOL
PAVED, THE GROUND OF YOUNG BODIES IMMIGRANT FOR STUDY.
REMEMBER *LES PHRERES SIMPLISTES, LE GRAND JEU!*

IN THE PLACES OF PURCHASE, I IDENTIFY NARRATION THROTTLED, THE ANSWERS
TO STUDIES OF THE SOCIAL SETTINGS AS PROBLEMATIC ENVIRONMENT PERSPIRED
OF RELIGIOUS EDUCATION, OR THE "FACTORY BLOW OUT."

ORIENTED TOWARD MATTERS OF THE COMMUNICATIVE I AM
OF THE "FOREIGN GROUP" NOT THE POPULAR ISRAELI,
NOT THE RAGE "PRIME-TIME," NOT THE BLESSED MURDER.

THIS IS THE SHOCK AND AWE: IT IS AGAIN FOR ME ALONE TO FIND NO UNION.

[FOR THE
RECORD]

USA First-Class

POSTCARD

USA First-Class

To compare vocabularies of language one is privileged a definite scheme of particularities. Disparity is compared with divergence in dreams and "attitudes."

But discrepant glossaries is only the introduction. Is best to hear the mouth this long the mute.

Senator Norm Coleman
2550 University Ave W,
Suite 100N
St. Paul, MN 55114

POSTCARD

OF THE DEFINITION SOCIAL:

- IT BUILDS RECIPROCAL. IT INDICATES THE MAIN
FUNCTION OF THE LANGUAGE IN ISLAM.

- AND IT HAS OTHER MEANS OF THE COOPERATION
BETWEEN THE LIVING:

  - WITNESS THE "TRIBE" OF THE WOLF.
  - BUT NOW THE "ARMY" OF BEES.

WE CANNOT FINISH OUR CLASSIFICATION
WITH LOS MUERTOS, BUT COLLABORATE
BEYOND "READING WRITING" WITH PHYSICAL
OBLIGATION: RAISED EYEBROWS? A NOD?

U.S. MISSION TO THE U.N.
140 EAST 45TH STREET
NEW YORK, N.Y. 10017

POSTCARD

Jesus, King of Beijing, Television should not oversee
the counter sales. Witness subliminal procedures
of the manufactured goods, the broken worker—
odds and ends, bits and pieces, rags and bones . . .

"Right." "Yeah." "Sure." I might differentiate in Hell
a brief oasis—but the Wal-Mart girl,
she "no can undertand" me—
"Bitch" and "I am speaking English" is no use.

Wal-Mart Supercenter
1550 Blake Avenue
Albert Lea MN 56007

POSTCARD

USA First-Class

EXAMPLE ANTIQUES—A COMBINATION WAREHOUSE PETROLEUM ON THE BORDER: THE MAN SELLS ELVIS VIVA LAS VEGAS (ORIGINAL 1964) VELVET TAPESTRY. $1.25 ON FRAME.

BUT NOT FOR ME. DIESES IST EIN VERBRECHEN. YOUR "KING OF ROCK AND ROLL" SANG FOR NIXON. TELL ME, IT IS TOO MUCH WE SOLICIT OUR CREATOR?

IT IS CERTAINLY THE EXCESS CHARGE OF THE DOOR REVOLVING: INFORMATION NOW IS BRITTANY SPEARS, NOW IS TEXAS, BUT IN YOUR MINNESOTA.

[IS OF NO USE]

POSTCARD

The simplification of domestic economic patterns is of no use to its subjects. The premise broken numbers of model behavior: all "dirt" must validate its position to beg participation in the crippling activities illuminating The Almighty Dog.

An arbitrary symbol without the necessary or natural connection with its meaning, the "White Buck" is rubbish meaning the same as the German "Hund," or the French "Chien," or the Latin "Canis." or "whatever" in your language, dominant friend.

I pay nothing to be trained. My dog is not for sale.

POSTCARD

USA First-Class

Says the alien Bob Perelman:

"Normal usage is the art
of channeling weapons
so the majority of sentences
willingly enforce
the current meaning of money
with a minimum of state body
revealed in the headlines"

Imagine a poetry assassinate its intended. This would
be of some use.

No matter, If I cannot be the good citizen, I will
settle for the money.

POSTCARD

Dream After <u>Das Buch der Bilder</u>

A call from a member of the distanced family as I moseyed cheer in a rose if temporary formal garden. A pleasant activity, watching the clouds, a metaphor to keep innocence from the childhood, I said, but it is old fast. Worse: they seem the flowers today, but don't I know what class. (This declaration first thing I thought I must add, to make my part in keeping connections familial.) I worked dutifully to describe clouds in paraphrases Rilkean: They need our fixed glances, I said. That one is why they form such flowers, sometimes the dragons or the faces of love we lacked. The clouds only wish to be noticed once, that they can die and not return again as clouds. He said that was lovely, "even in German."

POSTCARD

USA First-Class

RE: INVISIBILITY

ALTHOUGH TO HAVE THE SUITABLE LEVEL OF THE U.S. (ENGLISH)
BUSINESS ABILITY CAN BE CONSIDERED A WEAPON TO DEFEND
ITHE COMMUNICATIVE ENCOUNTER AS TRANSPIRES IN DIVERGENT SOCIAL ADJUSTMENTS,
THE ALIENS CANNOT "SALT AWAY" THE JUDGMENTS OF THE LANGUAGE BRACKETS.
EVEN IN THE SITUATIONS IN WHICH THE IMMIGRANT HUMANOIDS ——————
"LUCK OUT" LANGUAGE TO DEFEND, THE QUESTIONS OF INVISIBLE
POSSESSIONS ELUDES STANDARDIZED BLINDNESS TESTS. ——————

——————

DER AUSLÄNDER SIEHT MAN.
SIE SEHEN NICHT DIE AUSLÄNDER. ——————

IT IS TO PROCLAIM: THIS BOXED CARDBOARD IS MINE.
THIS WHOLE EMPTINESS IS MINE.

Be one of more than 68,000 dairy industry enthusiasts who make the trip to World Dairy Expo in Madison, Wisconsin. You'll find the most modern dairy equipment and the newest dairy technology and innovations, including animal health supplies, milking systems, feeding products, forage handling and manure equipment, plus embryos, semen and genetic research.

100 MILES FOR MADISON

MIST DRIPS DIESEL ENGINES IN THE DELLS.

FIVE HOURS OF MOONLIGHT SLEEPING WITH TRUCK DRIVERS.
DID NOT MOVE ANY THING IN THE CAR. CRAWLED ABOVE
THE PILE OF MY OBVIOUS BAGGAGE.

MORNING MILES IS THE FOG.   IS ONLY A CATTLE TRUCK.
STEEL BOX DOOR SLATTED. MOANING BLUE MADISON.

BLOATED RETURNS, SMOKEY FAT, SIX IN THE MORNING.
DREAMED THE ANSWER TO A QUESTION I FORGET.

WHY IN DAIRY COUNTRY I CANNOT FIND THE CREAM AUTHENTIC?

MONSANTO COMPANY
DAIRY/UPPER MIDWEST
2820 WALTON COMMONS
WEST - SUITE 100
MADISON, WI 53718

POSTCARD

DEVICE

FERTILIZE Y FERTILIZE Y FERTILIZE... DEAR CHILDREN,
COMPLEX SYSTEMS EATING THE WASTE CORPORATE,
SAY "THANK YOU." SAY NO BODEGA, NO PAGODA, NO MAS.
RIGID GEOMETRY FORCED IN VARIED CURVES IS "MOTHER,"
IS "NATURE," IS "SYSTEMATIC VIOLATION." MUY BUENO.
THIS DEVICE IS FOR YOU, THE MUTILATED OF NO ART.

POSTCARD

MIL-WAU-KEE

COULD HOPE HARDLY TO OBTAIN "BEGUN." THERE WERE QUESTIONS
OF NECESSARY WATERLILIES AND BIOGRAPHERS, THAT THEY
SCRATCHED OLD WOUNDED, BUT THE ANTICIPATION OF FRESH BREEZES OF THE
"PLEASANT LAND," IN THIS HELLFIRE MORNING AND "MUGGY TO BOOT," ADDED TO
THE ENTHUSIASM OF THE FINAL PREPARATIONS. I GLIDED TO VISIT ALL
THE SEGREGATIONS IN NINE HOURS. I WAS PREPARED EVERYTHING—EVEN MY SMALL
STICK WALKING ROBUST.

THE ADVENTURE AS BIOGRAPHERS HAD SLANDERED SMOOTHLY WAS FOR ANYTHING BUT.
"MILLIOKE." "MINWAKING." I DID NOT SEE MUCH MINGLING IN MIL-WAU-KEE.

THE AFFLICTION IS I. IT WANTED NOW TO PUT MY WINNEBAGO IN THE PERSISTENCE
STORE, IF IT HAS THE MONEY TO BURN ITSELF, OR SITE IN ITS HEART FOR ONE
MORE MEMORY OF MIL-WAU-KEE.

POSTCARD

Indiana

It is the mirrors identical in the line.
It is the pink soap porcelain convenience.
It is the clean and dry hands machine.

It is directive of parent to child:
"Don't touch!" "Come here!"

But it is also the silence between us.
Who will say they are the waste
smeared on the stall: "Allah eats shit"

Indiana State
Department of Health
2 N Meridian St
Indianapolis, IN 46204

Michigan Commission on Law Enforcement Standards and Education

Course #2109:

Spanish for Criminal Justice Response Professionals

Welcome to the classroom version of Spanish for Criminal Justice Response Professionals, a Spanish course designed for law enforcement and correctional custody officers. This course is designed to develop speaking and listening skills and to promote a deeper understanding of the Hispanic population in the state of Michigan. The utmost concern is to provide a foundation in the Spanish language that will not only lead to a strong repertoire for communicating with Spanish-speaking people, but also to the provision of officer safety.

Learning Objective 1.1

The student will be able to interpret the Spanish words and phrases that may signal danger as they are spoken within a conversation during a simulated response.

Spanish	English Translation
¡Policía!	Police!
¡Desármalo!	Disarm him!
¡Brincale!	Jump him!
¡Pégale!	Hit him!
¡Agarra el arma!	Grab his weapon!
¡Arráncate! or ¡Córtalo(la)	Cut him/her!
¡Pícalo!	Stab him!
¡Dispárale!/Tírele!	Shoot him!
¡Corre!	Run!

POSTCARD

POSTCARD

RADIO FATS

Who will care to flap the Alien Tongue?.

Pale, or charred, the words deserve excess of the negligible attention commonplace language permits. C'est un abattage.

The formation of the oration is a linguistic, isolable element of the content; most impervious characteristic or pulse of languages is style of the flexion. Example:

- "<u>You</u> are los diablo con ojos azules"; i.e., "He or she is not los diablo con ojos azules, you are."
- "You <u>are</u> los diablo con ojos azules"; i.e., "In case you thought you were not los diablo con ojos azules."

POSTCARD

USA First-Class

2825 MILES.

WELCOME TO OHIO: "SO MUCH TO DISCOVER!"

POSTCARD

USA First-Class

7:20 MEANS SITTING SIDE OF THE HIGHWAY, MY PIECES OF THE WINDOW, THE PAPER IN "MAGIC" MARKER:

¿ADÓNDE USTED VA?

OÙ ALLEZ-VOUS?

WOHIN GEHEN SIE?

WHERE ARE YOU GOING?

AYÚDEME, POR FAVOR.

AIDEZ-MOI, SVP.

HELFEN SIE MIR, BITTE.

HELP ME, PLEASE

IMAGINE SOON A MAN OF THE FORCE WILL STOP AND USE HIS HAND ON ME.

NEVER THE LESS I CONTENTED OF TIME FOR IMPROVE MY REWRITE OF <u>LANGUAGE OF A NATION: BIG AMERICAN TRIP.</u>

POSTCARD

USA First-Class

SAYS THE ALIEN ANTONIO MACHADO-RUIZ:

"THE 'OTHER' DOES NOT EXIST: THIS IS THE
CONCLUSION OF RATIONAL FAITH, THE INCURABLE
BELIEF OF HUMAN REASON . . . AS IF, IN
THE END, EVERYTHING MUST NECESSARILY AND
ABSOLUTELY BE 'ONE AND THE SAME.' BUT THE
'OTHER' REFUSES TO DISAPPEAR; IT SUBSISTS, IT
PERSISTS; IT IS THE HARD BONE ON WHICH REASON
BREAKS ITS TEETH."

ISRAELI EMBASSY
3514 INTERNATIONAL DR. N.W.
WASHINGTON DC 20008

POSTCARD

[ALLOW THAT IT IS CONFUSED OR ANGERED. I DO NOT
UNDERSTAND THE SYSTEM BUT MUST NAVIGATE THE SAME:]

TO PLEASE THE DEBATABLE POINT, THEIR VALUES MUST BE ORDERED BULK AND
WELDED ACCORDING TO CERTAIN BROKE-DOWN CHASSIS OF FORMS. NOBODY FEELS
SORRY OF ITS BROKEN WHEELS OR THE IMPOSSIBILITY OF THE NEW USE. NO EDITION
TO THEM IS. THIS INCLUDES NOT ONLY ONE BOG OR BEVY OF THE SYNONYMOUS
SOUNDS FOR "PRESTIDIGITATION" FOR "SLEIGHT OF HAND," BUT ALSO MOST OF OUR
TECHNICAL TERMINOLOGY. (& THEY WOULD DEMARCATE THIS CASE OF ROADSIDE WEEPING
WITH WORDS REGISTERED FOR ALL MOTORISTS TO SCRUTINIZE.)

[THE WORDS WHISPERED OF LENGTH AS INSOMNAMBULIST (AND MAGNIFIED IN TAR
OIL) ONLY ACCOMPANY SMEARING THEMSELVES FOR ALL ABOVE. PRESTIDIGITATION IS OF
THAT, MY FRIEND, WHEREVER YOU ARE, THIS NIGHT OF NO ECHOES ON WET ROADS.]

POSTCARD

A HOUSE, <u>WHICH</u> IS NOT NECESSARILY A HOME, MAY BE TOO EXPENSIVE, EVEN WHEN HOUSES <u>THAT</u> ARE NOT HOMES ARE EVERYWHERE FOR SALE.

I AM TIRED WITHOUT ONE MORE DAY A HOME.
I AM TIRED WITHOUT ONE MORE DAY A FRIEND.

MY HOME, WHICH IS NOT THE HOUSE, DOES NOT EXIST.

POSTCARD

I AM NOT THE CRUMPLED PYLON

I AM NOT THE BROKEN YELLOW LINE

I AM NOT GOING THE **WRONG WAY**

IT IS NOWHERE IT IS CLOSE

IT IS STILL DRIVELING IGNITED

IT IS TO PROJECT A PAST ONTO THE SLATE

IT IS WELCOME

IT IS THE EMPIRE STATE

IT IS A TARGET A SHINING A NEVERTHELESS

IT IS DO NOT PASS

IT IS ROUGH ROADS

IT IS SHOTGUNS

IT IS "BORED KIDS"

IT IS NYC 150 MILES

IT IS THE UPSTATE FOG

USA First-Class

POSTCARD

Comme Lou Reed dit, "Ils tueront vos fils."

The English language as each sad dog knows has a double vocabulary. Null system of terms lend to programs grinding "wheel of fortune" into "socioeconomic collapse."

Or suddenly subject matter is popular and calls for the precision warning, oaths, and finger-pointing.

Q: What of this "foreign-learned vocabulary?"
A: Cluster Bombs.
Q: And families, even little words loaned of alien languages?
A: Freedom Fries.

This cast abroad. This our transmission. This is "We."

USA First-Class

Press Secretary
The White House
1600 Pennsylvania Ave. NW
Washington, DC 20500

POSTCARD

THE FINAL CLAUSE
OF THE DEFINITION

IS THAT A LANGUAGE
CANNOT WORK

UNLESS THERE ARE TWO PEOPLE
TO SPEAK IT.

WHEN THERE IS ONLY ONE,
THE LANGUAGE IS PRONOUNCED

"DEAD."

POSTCARD

USA First-Class

You said these things in plain English:

"There is fatigue, something stagnant about the poetry
being written today. . . . When did you last read a poem
whose political vision truly surprised or challenged you?"

You invoked Homer Virgil Chaucer Wordsworth Dickinson
Whitman Pound Eliot Yeats Williams Moore Stevens.
You invoked Dana Gioia & Mary Oliver. And Stein?
Have you no irony, John Barr?

John Barr, you should not have invoked Stein.
She is none too pleased. She says there are no frauds
in death, and you will want to avoid her at dinnerparties.
John Barr, you have not read a word of the new poetries.
John Barr, get a bloody catalog from SPD.

John Barr, President
The Poetry Foundation
444 North Michigan Avenue
Suite 1850
Chicago, Illinois 60611-4034

POSTCARD

YOU SAID THESE THINGS IN PLAIN ENGLISH:

"WE NO LONGER COMMUNICATE."
"I DON'T UNDERSTAND YOU ANYMORE."
"YOU DON'T LISTEN TO ME WHEN I SPEAK."

YOU KNEW HOW TO "EXPRESS YOUR NEEDS" CLEARLY AND DIRECTLY. "WHEN YOU _____, I FELT _____." YOUR WORDS WERE TIRED. OR WE WERE TIRED. OR IT WAS TIRED. THE WORDS WERE TOO SIMPLE. I WOULD NOT "WORK ON OUR PROBLEMS." I STOPPED SPEAKING CORRECTLY. I STOPPED SPEAKING. "POSITIVE COMMUNICATION REQUIRES DIRECT, UNAMBIGUOUS STATEMENTS OF FEELING." WHEN YOU USED THESE WORDS I FELT NAUSEATED AND WEAK. I WANTED TO STICK A GUN IN MY MOUTH. WHICH IS NOT A FEELING, YOU WERE RIGHT IN SAYING. I DO NOT LOVE YOU/YOU HURT ME/I HURT YOU/I AM SORRY. I DO NOT MISS THESE WORDS. I DO NOT WANT TO FEEL THESE THINGS. I CANNOT MOVE FAR ENOUGH AWAY.

[CONSPICUOUS ABSENCE]

POSTCARD

USA First-Class

IT IS THE POSITIVE VIBRATION:

THE NATION OF BROOKLYN

IT IS APPARENTLY A COMMON FEELING, THE AGREEMENT OF THE BODEGA.

I HAVE PURCHASED THE SHIRT.

Maybe I WILL WALK THE BRIDGE.

NOTES

FOR THEIR EDITING &/OR SUPPORT, THE AUTHOR THANKS
COMRADES WEST & EAST, ELENA GEORGIOU, THE ENTIRE PHILPIN
CLAN, SELAH SATERSTROM, JULIANNA SPALLHOLZ, ZINNIA SU, &
THE FOLKS CURRENTLY SHOOTING VIDEOS FOR THIS PROJECT, WHOM I CAN'T
PRESENTLY NAME, DUE TO MY LIMITED PERCEPTION OF THE TIME-SPACE CONTINUUM.

MORE THANKS TO THE PATIENT TONY FRAZER & ALL AT SHEARSMAN BOOKS,
AND YET MORE TO THE EDITORS OF THE JOURNALS IN WHICH SECTIONS OF THIS
BOOK APPEARED, OFTEN IN VERY DIFFERENT FORMS: ACTION YES, EDITED BY
JOHANNES GÖRANSSON & JOYELLE McSWEENEY; BIRD DOG, EDITED BY SARAH
MANGOLD; FOURTEEN HILLS, EDITED BY JASON SNYDER, ET AL; PRACTICE: NEW
WRITING + ART, EDITED BY ADRIAN LURSSEN AND SUSAN TICHY; SHAMPOO,
EDITED BY DEL RAY CROSS; UNPLEASANT EVENT SCHEDULE, EDITED BY DANIEL
NESTER; AND WORD FOR/WORD, EDITED BY JONATHAN MINTON.

USA First-Class

<u>BIG AMERICAN TRIP</u> APPROPRIATES MATERIAL FROM THE FOLLOWING SOURCES:

2005 WASHINGTON ANNUAL STATISTICS BULLETIN. USDA/NATIONAL AGRICULTURAL STATISTICS SERVICE, WASHINGTON FIELD OFFICE.

AGRICULTURAL RESOURCE MARKETING CENTER. HTTP://WWW.AGMRC.ORG/AGMRC/COMMODITY/FRUITS/RASPBERRIES/

DYLAN, BOB. "IT'S ALL OVER NOW, BABY BLUE," FROM THE ALBUM <u>BRINGING IT ALL BACK HOME</u>. COLUMBIA RECORDS, 1965.

FOREIGNER. "HOT BLOODED," FROM THE ALBUM <u>DOUBLE VISION</u>. ATLANTIC RECORDS, 1978.

HIGHWATER, JAMAKE. <u>THE PRIMAL MIND: VISION AND REALITY IN INDIAN AMERICA</u>. MERIDIAN / SIGNET, 1982.

KAMPGROUNDS OF AMERICA (KOA) PRESS RELEASE, 2 JUNE 2004.

LEE, DOROTHY. <u>FREEDOM AND CULTURE</u>. PRENTICE HALL, 1959. QUOTED IN <u>THE PRIMAL MIND</u>, BY JAMAKE HIGHWATER.

Machado-Ruiz, Antonio. Quoted in Jean Franco, An Introduction to Spanish-American Literature; quoted in The Primal Mind

McKenna, Terence. "Ordinary Language, Visible Language and Virtual Reality." Appears online at Deoxy.org: The Deoxyribonucleic Hyperdimension. http://deoxy.org/t_langvr.htm. (No further citation available).

Medora, ND, Chamber of Commerce promotional material.

Meinig, D.W. "The Beholding Eye: Ten Versions of the Same Scene." From The Interpretation of Ordinary Landscapes: Geographical Essays, D.W. Meinig, Editor. Oxford University Press, 1979.

Mineral County, MT, Information and Commerce promotional material.

Monsters of Destruction. http://www.monstersofdestruction.com

Montana Vacation, Recreation, Accommodations and Travel Information Website, http://www.visitmt.com/

USA First-Class

Pa-ta Shan-jen, translated in "Lodgepole," from "Hunting," in
Myths & Texts, by Gary Snyder. Totem Press/Corinth Books, 1960.

Perelman, Bob. "State Heads," in Virtual Reality. Roof Books, 1993.

Strunk, William; and White, E.B. The Elements of Style. Fourth
Editon. Allyn and Bacon, 2000.

Sturtevant, E. H. Introduction To Linguistic Science. Yale University Press, 1966.

Sweet Grass County, MT, Chamber of Commerce promotional material.

Texas Commission on Law Enforcement Standards and Education.
HTTP://WWW.TCLEOSE.STATE.TX.US

Thoreau, Henry David, from "Brute Neighbors," in Walden. Quoted in the US
National Forest Campground Guide. HTTP://FORESTCAMPING.COM

Three Forks Chamber of Commerce promotional material.

USA First-Class

ABOUT THE AUTHOR

CHRISTIAN PEET IS THE AUTHOR OF TWO CHAPBOOKS/INSTALLMENTS OF AN ONGOING CROSS-GENRE PROJECT, THE NINES. HIS WORK APPEARS IN THE ANTHOLOGY, A BEST OF FENCE: THE FIRST NINE YEARS, AND IN JOURNALS SUCH AS ACTION YES, BIRD DOG, DENVER QUARTERLY, DRUNKEN BOAT, OCTOPUS MAGAZINE, PRACTICE: NEW WRITING + ART, AND SLEEPINGFISH, AMONG OTHERS. PEET LIVES IN VERMONT, IN THE U.S., WHERE HE RUNS TARPAULIN SKY PRESS, FREELANCES AS A BOOK AND WEB DESIGNER, AND TEACHES CREATIVE WRITING, POETRY, & LITERATURE AT THE COMMUNITY COLLEGE OF VERMONT. NOT UNLIKE THE POSTCARD-WRITER OF BIG AMERICAN TRIP, CHRISTIAN HAS DRIVEN ACROSS THE UNITED STATES HALF A DOZEN TIMES AND CAMPED IN ALL BUT FIVE STATES WHILE LIVING OUT OF HIS CAR AND ASSUMING A VARIETY OF EMPLOYEE INCARNATIONS INCLUDING PRODUCE AISLE GUY, SHEET METAL FABRICATOR, GOAT MILKER, ORGANIC SPROUT GROWER, MAINTENANCE MAN, LANDSCAPER, AND CONVENIENCE STORE CLERK.

USA First-Class